1 Big Tree

Name   Date

To parents   First your child will practice scribbling. Even if your child does not choose a green crayon, allow him or her to proceed. Praise your child when he or she has completed the

≪ **example** ≫

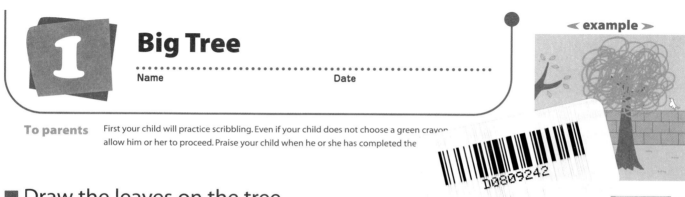

green ➤

■ Draw the leaves on the tree.

Blue Sky

‹ example ›

■ Draw the clouds on the sky.

white ▷

Walk on the Field

Name

Date

To parents From this page on, your child will practice filling in a white area. The color of the sample crayon is just a reference. If you don't have the same crayon, it is okay to use a similar color or any color your child likes.

■ Color the white circle.

< **example** >

blue ▶

To parents In this exercise your child will practice drawing lines and improve his or her crayon control skills. It is okay for your child to choose a crayon that he or she likes.

■ Draw a line from the arrow (↓) to the star (★) by connecting each ⬤.

< example >

■ Color the white circle.

`yellow`

■ Draw a line from the arrow (↓) to the star (★) by connecting each .

To parents   The white square is designed to draw your child's attention to the shape of the slide. Encourage your child to color along the inside edges of the white square first, and then fill in the middle area.

≺ example ≻

■ Color the white square.

violet ▶

■ Draw a line from the arrow (↓) to the star (★) by connecting each .

5 Swing

Name   Date

To parents   First show your child how to color inside the edges of the white section, and then move to the middle. If he or she seems to be having difficulty, show your child what to do.

≺ example ≻

■ Color the white rectangle.

orange ▶

■ Draw a line from the arrow (↓) to the star (★) by connecting each 🧺.

Water the Plants

Name

Date

To parents   Your child will practice coloring a triangular area in this exercise. Encourage your child to color the inside edges of the white triangle first, and then complete the middle portion.

< example >

■ Color the white triangle.

red

■ Draw a line from the arrow (↓) to the star (★) by connecting each .

Rabbits

Name

Date

To parents Don't be concerned about coloring over the edges. What is most important is that your child enjoys coloring.

■ Color the white triangle.

≺ example ≻

brown ▶

■ Draw a line from the arrow (↓) to the star (★) by connecting each 🐰.

8 Running

To parents   From this page on, your child will practice coloring several areas in each exercise. On this page, there are two blank areas. Encourage your child to color both areas.

■ Color the white circles.

‹ example ›

green ▶ orange ▶

■ Draw a line from the arrow (↓) to the star (★) by connecting each 👕.

9 Sandbox

Name

Date

To parents When your child has finished this page, compare it with his or her previous work. If you notice any progress, offer lots of praise, such as, "You're really getting good!"

‹ example ›

blue ▶ violet ▶

■ Color the white circle and square.

■ Draw a line from the arrow (↓) to the star (★) by connecting each 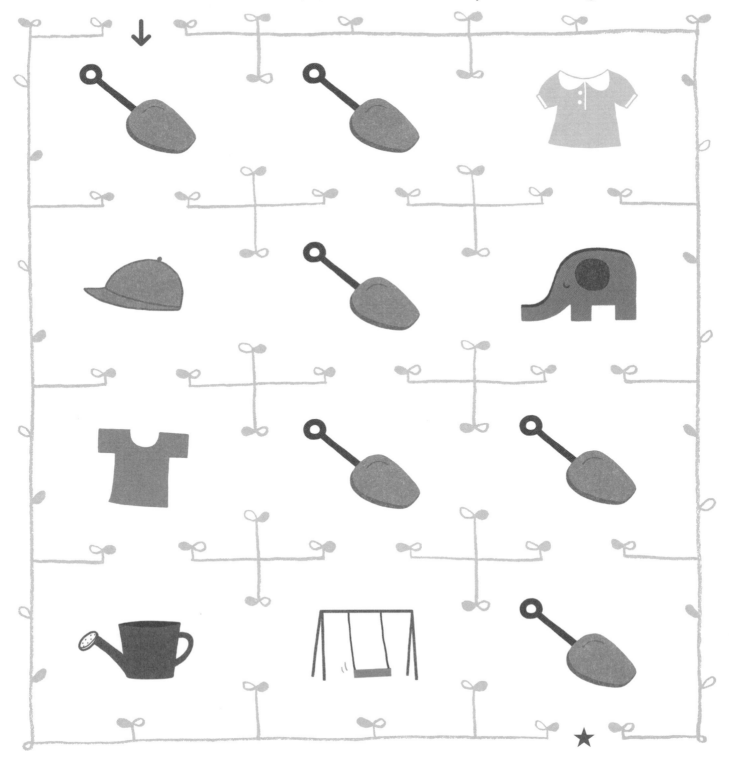.

Playing Ball

Name

Date

To parents Your child will use three colors on this page. If he or she seems to be having difficulty, you can help choose the crayon by asking, "What is the color of each ball?"

■ Color the white circles and triangle.

≺ example ≻

blue ▶ orange ▶ red ▶

■ Draw a line from the arrow (↓) to the star (★) by connecting each ⬤.

To parents It is important that your child becomes aware of shapes and colors. Talk with your child about the different shapes and colors in this illustration.

< example >

■ Color the white circle, triangle and square.

green ▶ orange ▶ yellow

To parents From this page on, the maze activities become more complex.
If your child is having difficulty, please guide your child by asking,
"Where is the next green t-shirt?" When your child has completed
the exercise, praise his or her hard work.

■ Draw a line from the arrow (↓) to the star (★) by connecting each 👕.

Big Blocks

Name   Date

To parents There are four white areas that your child will color on this page. Ask your child to choose which four colors he or she wants to use. It is okay if the colors your child chooses are different than the colors in the example.

< example >

■ Color the white circles and squares.   brown ▶ red ▶ violet ▶ yellow ▶

■ Draw a line from the arrow (↓) to the star (★) by connecting each 🏠.

13 **Rainy Day**

Name   Date

≪ example ≫

■ Color the white circles, triangle and square.

blue ▸ orange ▸ red ▸ yellow ▸

■ Draw a line from the arrow (↓) to the star (★) by connecting each 🌂.

14 Pool

Name   Date

To parents If you have been to a pool together, talk with your child about the fun time you had as he or she colors the picture.

< example >

■ Color the white circle, triangles and square.

blue ▷ orange ▷ red ▷ yellow ▷

■ Draw a line from the arrow (↓) to the star (★) by connecting each ▢.

Lunchbox

Name

Date

To parents There are five white areas that your child will color on this page. When your child has finished, talk about his or her favorite food in this lunchbox.

≪ example ≫

■ Color the white circles,
triangle and squares.

| brown ▶ | green ▶ | orange ▶ | red ▶ | yellow ▶ |

■ Draw a line from the arrow (↓) to the star (★) by connecting each 🍪.

16 Chicken

Name

Date

To parents From this page on, each exercise will require more careful coloring. In this exercise, your child will color only one section.

< example >

■ Color the chicken's comb.

red

■ Draw a line from the arrow (↓) to the star (★) by connecting each 🐔.

Concert

Name

Date

To parents Your child will color the drum in this picture. When your child is finished, you can talk about his or her favorite instrument.

< example >

■ Color the drum.

brown ▶

■ Draw a line from the arrow (↓) to the star (★) by connecting each .

18 Toy Box

Name

Date

To parents   Your child will color the toy ship in this picture. When he or she is finished, say, "What a good boy! He is putting his toys away."

< example >

■ Color the ship.

black ▶

■ Draw a line from the arrow (↓) to the star (★) by connecting each 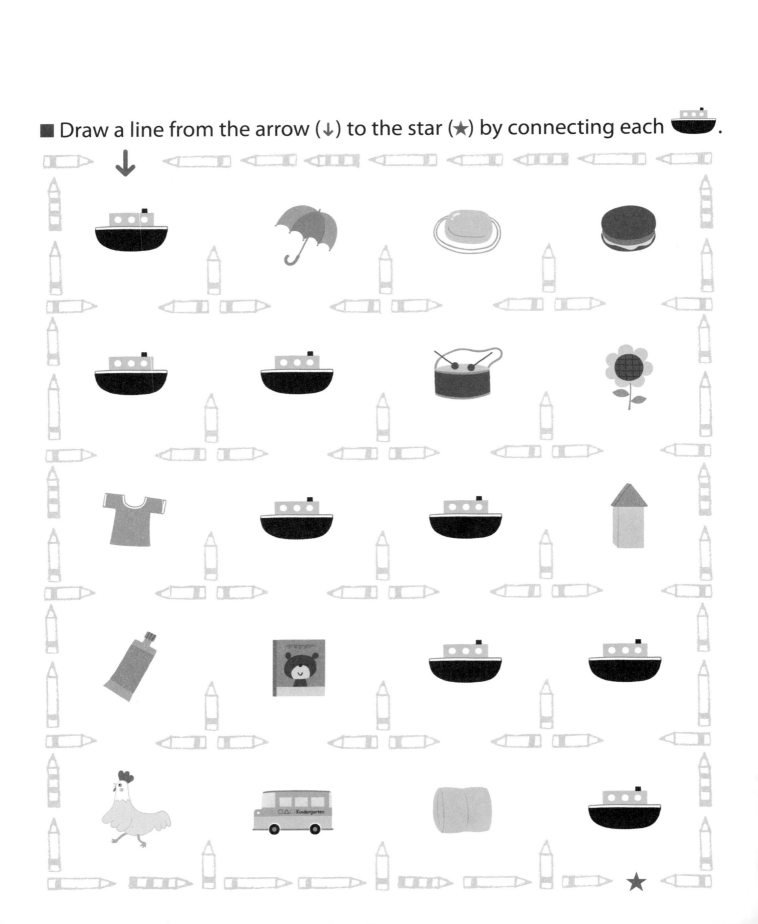.

Library

Name .... Date ....

■ Color the picture books.

≪ example ≫

blue ▶   red ▶

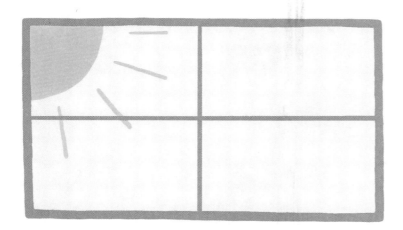

■ Draw a line from the arrow (↓) to the star (★) by connecting each .

20 Clean Up

Name

Date

To parents When your child has finished this page, offer lots of praise. You can say, "Good kids wash their hands often—just like you do, too."

■ Color the towel and soap.

‹ example ›

green ▶ yellow ▶

To parents   From this page on, the maze activities become more intricate. If your child is having difficulty, please guide your child by asking, "Where is the next yellow bar of soap?" When your child has completed the exercise, praise his or her hard work.

■ Draw a line from the arrow (↓) to the star (★) by connecting each .

21 **Brush Your Teeth**

Name   Date

To parents   Your child will color the cup and toothpaste. When your child completes this page, you can say, "What a good boy! He is brushing his teeth before bed. You brush your teeth then, too."

< example >

■ Color the cup and toothpaste.

blue ▶ yellow ▶

■ Draw a line from the arrow (↓) to the star (★) by connecting each 🧴.

School Bus

Name

Date

To parents   The area your child will color is larger than the previous page. When he or she has finished, offer lots of praise, such as, "Wow! You colored a lot."

■ Color the bus.

≪ example ≫

black ▶ yellow ▶

■ Draw a line from the arrow (↓) to the star (★) by connecting each 🚌.

Sunflowers

Name

Date

To parents Your child will color sunflowers. The white areas are intricate. If he or she colors outside the lines, it is okay.

≪ example ≫

■ Color the sunflowers.

brown ▶ yellow ▶

■ Draw a line from the arrow (↓) to the star (★) by connecting each 🌻.

24 Valentine's Day

Name   Date

< example >

■ Color the hearts.

red ▶ violet ▶ yellow

■ Draw a line from the arrow (↓) to the star (★) by connecting each ●.

Birthday Cake

Name   Date

To parents   Your child will color a birthday cake in this picture. When he or she is coloring, you can say, "What kind of cake do you like?"

≪ example ≫

■ Color the cake.

red   ▶   yellow

■ Draw a line from the arrow (↓) to the star (★) by connecting each ●.

To parents From this page on, your child can choose any colors he or she likes. It is also okay to use a single color. Encourage your child to color independently until he or she is finished.

‹ example ›

■ Color the paper airplanes with your favorite colors.

■ Draw a line from the arrow (↓) to the star (★) by connecting each .

To parents   On this page, your child will color the kites. Your child can choose a different color for each shape or kite, or use his or her favorite color for them all. Encourage your child to color independently.

≺ example ≻

■ Color the kites with your favorite colors.

■ Draw a line from the arrow (↓) to the star (★) by connecting each ▲.

Hiking

Name

Date

To parents Don't be concerned if your child is coloring outside of the lines. Let your child be creative with the colors he or she uses.

≺ **example** ≻

■ Color the hats and tree trunks with your favorite colors.

■ Draw a line from the arrow (↓) to the star (★) by connecting each ■.

29 Trick or Treat

Name

Date

To parents Your child will color the Halloween costume. When he or she has finished, offer lots of praise.

■ Color the Halloween costume with your favorite colors.

■ Draw a line from the arrow (↓) to the star (★) by connecting each ■.

Santa Claus

Name   Date

To parents   This picture shows Santa Claus and a reindeer. When your child is finished, talk about the different winter holidays.

‹ example ›

■ Color the picture with your favorite colors.

■ Draw a line from the arrow (↓) to the star (★) by connecting each ◆.

31 New Year's Eve

Name

Date

< example >

■ Color the picture with your favorite colors.

■ Draw a line from the arrow (↓) to the star (★) by connecting each ◆.

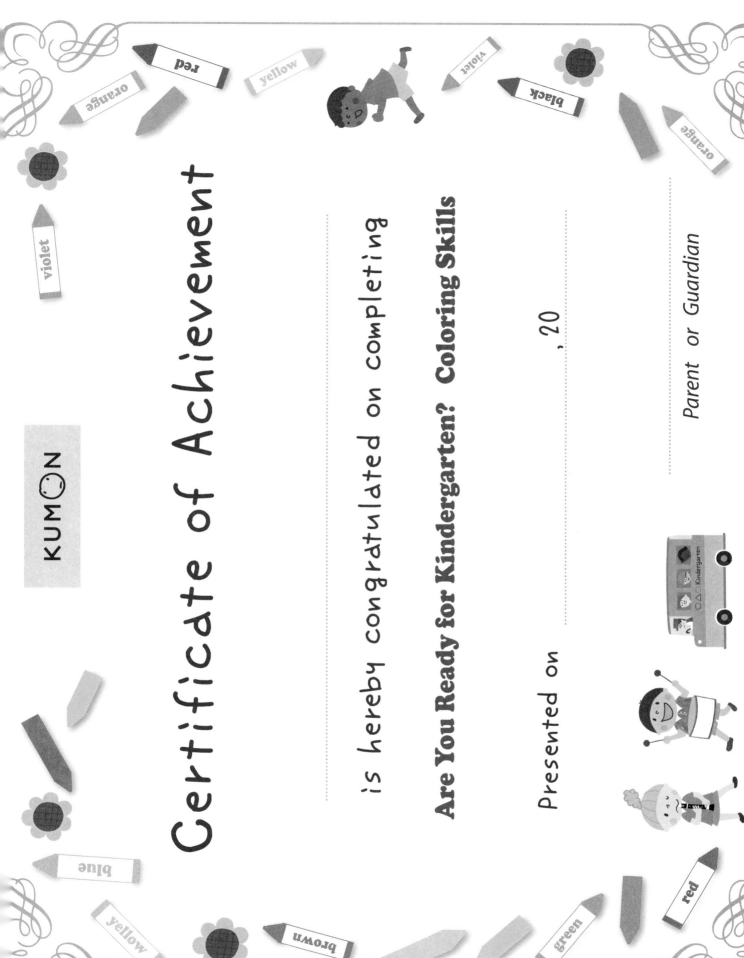

Certificate of Achievement

KUM◯N

is hereby congratulated on completing

Are You Ready for Kindergarten? Coloring Skills

Presented on _____ , 20 ____

_____
Parent or Guardian